MW00769129

Sister Stories
Revealing The Spirit Of Sisterhood

Compiled by Tricia Eleogram
Photographed by Louise Palazola
Designed by Stacey Berry

GUILD BINDERY PRESS

Sister Stories: Revealing The Spirit Of Sisterhood. Printed in the United States of America. Copyright ©1996 by Sisters Day Council, Inc. All rights reserved under International Copyright Law. Contents and/or cover may not be reproduced in whole or in part in any form without express written consent of the Publisher. Photography © Louise Palazola.

ISBN 1-55793-069-4

Library of Congress Cataloging-In-Publication Data

Sister Stories: Revealing The Spirit Of Sisterhood— 1st ed.

p.   cm.

1. Sisterhood–Stories and Anecdotes

2. Family– Inspirational and Motivational

First printing

10   9   8   7   6   5   4   3   2   1

Multiple copies of *Sister Stories* may be purchased at special discounts for fundraising, educational or sales promotion use. Contact the Sisters' Day Council at 666 Hawthorne, Memphis, Tennessee 38107 (901) 725-5190.

The Sisters' Day Council exists to provide and promote opportunities for siblings nationwide, to show appreciation for their sisters and give recognition to these important women from all segments of the community and to encourage positive and enjoyable relationships between all family members through the spirit of sisterhood and to enhance the growth of children, volunteers, parents and guardians, through educational activities that support caring, trust and friendship among siblings.

Sisters' Day is celebrated the first Sunday in August and is recognized by *Chase's Calendar of Events.*

Editor and Publisher: Randall J. Bedwell
Managing Editor: Palmer Jones
Layout & Design: Stacey Berry, Partners In Design, 6771 Bainbridge Dr. , Memphis, Tennessee 38119 (901) 755-0751/Fax: (901) 754-9923.

Guild Bindery Press, Inc.
Post Office Box 38099
Germantown, Tennessee 38183
e-mail guildmedia@aol.com

This book is dedicated to the Carroll sisters - Libby, Angela and Amy.
May the spirit of sisterhood live on.

INTRODUCTION

———— ❧ ————

It has become an annual tradition during my girls weekend-getaways for my friends and I to update each other on our sisters' lives. We have come to realize that although the degree of closeness varies, the bond between sisters is universally felt. Building on this notion, we began collecting anecdotes that reveal the spirit of sisterhood. Some made us laugh, others touched our hearts. As we gathered, several themes quickly emerged:

Sisters and Clothes, Sisters on Vacation, Sisters as Roommates and Sisters on the Telephone.

Because sisters often overlook differences, forgive past arguments and accept idiosyncrasies with understanding and laughter, their relationships withstand the test of time. The unique characteristics of sisterhood are revealed in the pages of this book. These stories may help you recall a special moment you've shared with your own sister.

Take time to celebrate sisterhood. This August join sisters nationwide by taking part in Sisters' Day and establish the tradition of honoring each other for years to come.

THE DATING GAME

THE DATING GAME

Lord help the mister who comes between me and my sister.

In the early 1970s, when my sister, Mandy, and I were around 14 or 15 years old, my father bought a 42-acre farm in Greers Ferry, Arkansas, population 272. He would take us up there and threaten to move the whole family to the farm to live. Dad was sure that if we just got to know some of the teenagers who lived around there, we would love it. That was when he set us up with two boys he met at the marina, Royce and Leroy. They came to get us in their pickup truck. Dad was so pleased that we were getting involved. My sister and I, two city girls, were prepared to be bored to death as we pulled up to the local Dairy Queen hangout. Later that night, we were surprised and frightened when Royce and Leroy took us down a dark country road to the local bootlegger's house, who, thankfully, had run out of beer. We were even more terrified when we found ourselves drag-racing through the Ozark Mountains screaming with fear and excitement.

❧

My sister Ellen used to date a guy who would come to our house every afternoon to visit her. He would make himself at home on the living room couch watching TV. He always took his shoes off to get comfortable. The smell of his feet would clear the room. My sisters and I had to pull Ellen out of the room and tell her to ask him to put on his shoes. PUGH!

When my older sister began to date, I was very curious about what all this "dating" entailed. One evening, when my sister's date arrived, I sneaked out to his car while he was in the house with her and my parents. Because of the enormous amount of junk on the floorboard of this 19-year-old young man's back seat, hiding was difficult, and I was certain I would be caught the moment they got in the car. Much to my surprise, they didn't even notice me. They started down the street, talking about the fancy restaurant where we were headed. As we turned the first corner, I began to get nervous. What was I doing? After the next turn, I jumped up and yelled, "Surprise!" My sister was very angry and so was her date. He put the car in reverse, and as I kept telling them, "I just wanted to see what a date was like," he *backed* the car all the way to my house.

Blind date, double date, no date … Which would you prefer?

VANITY FAIR

Vanity Fair

Sisters and bathrooms are like oil and water. They don't mix.

Out of the three of us, only one was blessed with a talent for hairstyling. During the late Fifties, Sue would tease our hair way up on top of our heads like a beehive. I remember the three of us in the bathroom together with the Spray Net. We could hardly breathe! I also have vivid memories of a wicked hairbrush fight between my two sisters.

❧

When I was a toddler, my older sister Faith bathed me. On one particular day when we were bathing, my mom left the door to the house open to get some fresh air. Faith had to get out of the tub to get the soap. This was a perfect opportunity to make a run for it. By the time Faith returned with the soap, I was already running out the door.

❧

Growing up, my sister, Sharon, and I shared the bathroom between our two rooms. When taking a shower, I would lock both doors, the one leading to my room and the one leading to her room. Frequently, I would leave the bathroom and inadvertently forget to unlock the door leading to Sharon's room. She became very frustrated because she would have to walk around through my room to enter the bathroom, so she started locking my door to the bathroom on purpose. This became an ongoing battle until my mother finally put a stop to it, after I securely taped Sharon's door and doorknob with duct tape.

Donna and her friends were very quiet when they locked the bathroom door and made their secret plans. I could hear them whispering and giggling, but I didn't have a clue as to their secrets. It wasn't until later that I found out.

I was completely in the dark the day my sister put on my brand-new dress and tried to leave the house. I chased after her and tried to stop her from leaving. After all, I had not had the chance to wear it yet. I was yelling at her as she went out the front door. What I didn't know was that she was running off to get married. After we found out what she had done, our mother was certain that I knew what Donna was up to that day and didn't tell. I don't think I've ever convinced her that all I wanted was my dress.

We grew up in a small house with everyone using one bathroom, so there was very little privacy. I noticed my older sister, Claudia, was in the bathroom with the door open, and I decided this would be the perfect time for one of my practical jokes. Our brother, Bubba, was a baby at the time, so I wrapped up my doll in a big blanket to look like Bubba. Then I walked down the hall right in front of the bathroom door and pretended to trip. The doll went flying out of my arms, and I screamed, "Bubba!" Claudia's eyes got as big as saucers and she started yelling for Mama. It didn't take her long to figure out it was a joke, with me rolling on the floor laughing.

Hairspray, bubble bath and duct tape …

WHILE YOU WERE SLEEPING

While You Were Sleeping

Now I lay me down to sleep, does your sister have cold feet?

My sister had a wonderful sense of humor. I remember when I went to Europe for the first time, she came by the house and put pillows under the covers on my bed and put my wig on the pillow at the head of the bed. When my husband came home, he thought I had returned and was asleep in bed. She laughed at the joke she had played on him.

Most people would think that the "big sister" would be the strong, brave one in the family. That was not the case in our house. My sister is three years younger than I and is not afraid of anything. Believe it or not, when I was a senior in high school, I would come home from work or a date late in the evening, and even though I had my own room with my own nice, cozy bed, I would always sneak into her room and tell her to "scoot over." I was sleeping in her bed for the night. As usual, she would always make room for me (even though she would laugh).

Now that we are both grown and married with children of our own, I am still considered the "chicken" of the family. When my husband goes out of town, I call my sister and pack my bag (along with my daughters') and head to her house. Fortunately, I have overcome a little bit of my fear and am now capable of sleeping in the spare bedroom by myself. I don't think my brother-in-law would appreciate me telling him to "scoot over."

I prepared the guest bedroom for my sister and her son for the weekend. When they arrived late that night, my 2-year-old nephew was fussy and didn't want to go to bed. I told my sister to go on to sleep and I would lie down on the couch with the baby. I awoke, on the couch, about 2:30 a. m. and put the baby in the guest bed. While I was tucking him in, my sister got up to use the bathroom. When I went to get in bed, I found that she had crawled into my bed with my husband and both of them were sound asleep. As I tried to awaken my sister, she said, "Leave me alone. Get out of my room!" I quickly explained that she was in MY room and in MY bed with MY husband. She barely opened her eyes as I led her back to the guest room. My husband slept through the whole thing without a clue.

The conversation over coffee the next morning had my husband at a loss for words. This isn't what Mother had in mind when she told us to share.

I was 8 years old when Jenifer was born, and I immediately took on the role of "Little Mother." When Jen was 2 years old, our mother decided it was time to move her from the baby bed into the bed with her big sister. There was only one drawback with this move. Because of Jen's occasional bed-wetting problem, Mom put a plastic sheet on my bed to protect the mattress. Have you ever been on a plastic sheet when a 2-year-old wets the bed? Guess what happens to the puddle. It rolls to the heaviest person in the bed, and that was me. I can remember many a night, scooping up my sleeping sister, changing her clothes and sitting her in the rocking chair beside the bed. Her little head would bob back and forth as she slept in the chair while I changed the bed linen. Needless to say, this was not a pleasant experience for me. After about a month of being soaked at least three times a week, I was aiming at the rocking chair and hoping my sister would land in it when I tossed her in that direction. This problem was finally rectified when our mother decided it would be safer to invest in twin beds.

Pillows, wigs and plastic sheets … No one ever fell asleep.

SISTER SENIOR

SISTER SENIOR

Sisterhood may be a "sting operation."

Merlynn is seven years older than I am. Apparently, at age 6, I would do anything for her. She used to tell me that I was her best friend and that she wanted me to sleep over. She would have me pack my suitcase and go outside to ring the doorbell of my own house. Sometimes I had to ring it many times before she would answer the door. Merlynn would pretend to show me around the house and then take me to her room, like I had never seen it before. The things I would do for my sister! It probably took me until age 10 before I wised up.

⁂

I have always thought my sister, Denise, was the coolest person in the world. I am three years younger, but that never seemed to matter to her. When she had her friends over to spend the night, I was almost always welcome to sit in on the all-night chatter sessions, as long as I kept my mouth closed. Being around my sister and her friends made me feel like I was one of the older girls. I only remember having to listen from outside my sister's bedroom door a few times.

⁂

I remember riding the Spider at the fair one time when I was about 5 years old and Lynn was 8. As the Spider spun around, its legs would move in and out, thrusting occupants together on one side of its compartments. When I entered the gate to get on the ride, all of the compartments were full except the seat next to my sister. She did ***not*** want me riding with her, but I climbed in anyway. I remember the disgusted look on her face as she said in her meanest 55-pound Terminator voice, "Don't touch me!" I clung to the side for dear life.

My older sister has always been known for "working her deal." One of her earlier scams involved our Easter baskets. After eating most of the candy in her basket, she demonstrated how we could combine our candy and have more candy for both of us. I fell for it. And I thought the Easter Bunny was fast!

ॐ

When Ashlee had her third birthday, I was unable to attend her party because I was out of town. As an adult without children at the time, I grossly underestimated the impact of my absence. Ashlee, now 9, still asks me occasionally, "Remember that time you didn't come to my birthday party, Ninny?" I feel sure she will remind me of this even when she's 30.

ॐ

Years ago in the 1930s, it was always a treat when my mother would give my sister and I each a penny. Mary would hold my hand as we walked to the corner store to pick out our penny candy. I guess I was about 3 years old and Mary was 6. We usually chose Black Cows.

One summer day when Mother gave us our pennies, Mary and I went out on the porch to swing before walking to the store. As we were slowly swinging, Mary started to sing softly. It was a warm day, and she began to rub my back very gently. My eyes started to close while we swung back and forth, back and forth, and I began to relax as she gently tickled my back. When I relaxed and fell asleep, I loosened my grip on my precious penny. Mary quietly removed it from my tiny palm and left me sleeping while she walked to the store without me. This little routine went on time after time, and I remember telling my mother, "Mary has the most beautiful tickle." It wasn't until I was much older that I realized what was happening.

I laugh when I remember the time I became aware of the "Older Sister Strategy." You know the classic line, "You do what I say or I'll tell!" It usually is unsheathed when the younger sister gets involved in some sort of little mishap, and the older sister convinces her that she'll be in SO much trouble if their parents find out. Of course, the older sister is willing to keep this secret in return for the popular, "Do anything I say."

In the late Sixties, my older sister showed me how to light those little incense cones that smelled so good. Strawberry was our favorite. To light them, you had to hold the flame on the cone for a while before they got started. Once when I was doing this, I didn't notice that the match was scorching the little flowered lamp shade on our precious porcelain lamp. Needless to say, my sister was going to tell on me because we had been warned never to play with fire. I begged her not to tell and she agreed, on the condition that I would do anything she wanted. For months and months, she made me do whatever she asked, which sometimes led to my getting in trouble. Finally I went to my mother and told her what I had done myself.

This stays so fresh in my memory. I now laugh because I realize the best thing about sisters when you get older is that they still know your secrets, but they keep them for free.

I was the first born of 10 children, and I dreamed of the day I would have a sister. I had almost given up hope after the five little brothers that followed me. Then along came Liz. Finally a sister! Boy was she a pest! I used to beg Mom and Dad for a padlock for my door because my room was irresistible for my little sister, 11 years younger than I. She had a ball dancing on top of my desk and scratching my records. She once buried my jewelry in the back yard, and some of it was never recovered. The age difference became less important as we grew and began to have more in common. I laugh because now Liz has a daughter with four younger brothers that followed her.

Growing up, my sister was as strong as an ox. She was constantly beating on me. If it weren't for my brother teaching me his brilliant technique of self-defense (lie on your back and kick like hell), I never would have survived. She was also very convincing. Once, she locked us in the bathroom and cajoled me into telling her what her Christmas present was. "If you tell me, I'll tell you," she said. We exchanged information, but on Christmas morning I discovered the deception. She had lied!

ॐ

I remember the Christmas when I was 10 years old, I wanted a Cabbage Patch doll. I was the first to wake up that Christmas morning and was excited to see two Cabbage Patch dolls under our Christmas tree. I thought both of the dolls were mine, but one was for my sister. One was a girl and the other a boy, but I liked the clothes the boy was wearing better. They looked just alike except for their clothing. Because I wanted the girl but liked the boy's clothes, I switched the certificates so my doll had the girl's name and Holly's had the boy name. Holly was only 4 years old and never knew the difference.

Bribery, scams and cons ... What took so long to figure it out?

IN THIS CORNER

IN THIS CORNER

Call the locksmith, call the pound. Where can a referee be found?

Doing house chores is still not one of my favorite activities, but growing up I dreaded it. When my sister was ready to begin her afternoon chores, somehow she felt that I should get motivated too. She would pester me and bug me until I just couldn't stand it any more. I had three hours before Mom was due home, and I wasn't getting started until I had to. When she went into the basement, where the washer and dryer were located, I locked her inside. Then I had to turn the radio up really loud so that I could enjoy "my time" without that annoying banging and screaming coming from the basement.

ॐ

As teenagers, my oldest sister, Pam, and I used to sit on the bed, rolling our hair every night. It would take about 30 minutes and at least 30 rollers each. I remember one night, my sister chased me and grabbed at my hair screaming, "That's my roller!"

ॐ

My sister, Geri, and I were born 23 months apart–she with a hard-driving, purposeful personality and I with a confused, people-pleasing personality. All our lives, she directed and fought for me. As a child, if anyone hurt me, they would have to answer to her. It was along about my 35th year when I realized I might be able to make my own decisions. I do remember one time when Geri could no longer listen to my piano practicing. You know, those monotonous scales and chords. That was when she closed the lid of the piano on my exercising fingers.

To this day, the mention of the words "Yellow Pages" makes me a little light-headed. It's all due to my sister, who today is my best friend but in years past was my mortal enemy. My job as a child was to pester my younger sister. Jill was very passive and reserved, so it was always a challenge to get her lathered up.

One day, Jill was watching TV in her rocking chair, minding her own business. (She happened to have a crush on Greg Brady.) I began my usual assault with loud off-key singing and animal noises made with my arm pits. After several minutes, my antagonism was getting to her. Finally, I got a "STOP IT!" out of her. My challenge was to break her down before Mom came out from the back. Mom was a gentle woman, but she had a mean streak a mile wide. My next weapon was incessant staring accompanied by lip smacking. It only took a couple of minutes to get a "QUIT IT! LEAVE ME ALONE!" My plan was working perfectly. Jill was getting agitated and Mom was none the wiser. One more irritation would put her over the edge. I resorted to a tried-and-true torture method–the rocking chair shake. I approached her from behind and furiously shook her rocking chair. Jill screamed at me to stop. Suddenly, from the rear of the house, we heard, "Girls. Stop. If one of you gets hurt, don't come running to me!" I sat smugly on the couch, trying not to burst into laughter. Jill sat in her chair, quietly brooding. She had an intense look on her face, a look that was very unfamiliar to me.

After several minutes, she rose deliberately and went behind me into the kitchen. I was enjoying I Love Lucy, when suddenly, WHAM! Everything went dark. After brief unconsciousness, I awoke and put my eyeballs back in their sockets. As the focus returned, I saw my quiet sister standing over me, holding the Yellow Pages over her head, ready to lower the whammy on me again. By this time, Mom was in full fury, grabbing Jill and yelling at us to behave. My head was a little sore, but Jill was the one who got in trouble. You never know when off-key singing can push someone over the edge.

ॐ

You've heard of teenage sisters fighting over the telephone. After repeatedly asking, then telling my sister to "get off the phone," I stuck her in the leg with a screwdriver. I was in serious trouble back then, but we laugh about it now. When I say, "I need the phone" to my children, they know I mean business.

In the Sixties, we used to use a straightening comb on our hair. Because there were four sisters and one comb, there was always an argument over who would use it first. I remember my two older sisters, Carol and Velma, scuffling over the comb. To this day, Velma has a scar on her face from that fight. No man has ever come between us, but don't ever mention the straightening comb around the four of us.

ॐ

As roommates during college, my sister and I shared the bathroom much more maturely than we had growing up. The problem with our living arrangement then was a cute little cocker spaniel named Katie. You see, my sister didn't really have time to train Katie (as if one can train a cocker spaniel). She was busy with college, work, and visiting her boyfriend at another school. Every weekend this hyper puppy was left behind for me to attend. She just assumed that I would take care of the puppy, and I was offended by this aimless arrangement. So I began to scoop up the poop the untrained puppy left behind, place it on the floor of my sister's room and close the door. Yes, I was right! There's nothing like puppy poo on one's bedroom floor to get one's attention.

When looking for an objective opinion, don't look at your sister.

DANGER ZONE

Danger Zone

It's true what they say, "Most accidents happen closest to home."

When we were 3, my twin sister and I were playing on the swivel bar stools. I was twirling her around when she fell to the floor and knocked out her front tooth. Even to this day she swears she saw the Tooth Fairy while she was at the dentist under the influence of the gas. Back then she described her in detail, complete with a long white chiffon dress and an ornate wand. I was so impressed! My sister had really seen the Tooth Fairy.

ॐ

Once Liz and I attended the same concert separately, each with our own set of friends. It just so happened that we both had a little too much to drink and came home nauseated. Liz, however, insisted that she had only had one glass of wine, so someone must have spiked it. My parents called the paramedics and pampered Liz, thinking that she had been poisoned. I, on the other hand, was scolded and left to deal with my self-inflicted torture on my own. Little did my parents know, Liz would have said anything to avoid being punished.

ॐ

My sister, Stacey, and I got into "hot water" a couple of times while we were growing up. But, I have to admit, the very first time was my fault.

When I was 5, I decided to get Stacey out of her crib (something my mother had told me never to do). As I climbed up and leaned over to get her out, I tripped over the cord to the hot water vaporizer. The vaporizer fell and burst, spilling hot water all over the hardwood floors. As I stood there with Stacey in my arms, the hot water began to soak through the feet of my footie pajamas. That's when I dropped her and jumped onto the bed. I believe this has something to do with Stacey's inability to stand still.

I'll never forget the time I stuck a holly berry in my ear. I had to be rushed to the doctor to have it removed. My sister, Rita, decided she would go along for the ride and watch me have it extracted, presumably to make me feel stupid. However, she was not pleased to find out that she was behind on her immunizations. Her little trip to the doctor "for fun" turned out to be not so fun after all.

৵

When the tough Italian boys down the street were mean to me, somehow my petite 78-pound sister managed to pull one of these tall wrestling team members into the gravel face-first. On my 16th birthday, while Denise was out of town, she allowed me to drive her shiny black sports car to school. I had an ever-so-slight, but ever-so-traumatic $673 fender bender that my sister has not mentioned again to this day.

Is there a doctor in the house?

GOING PLACES

GOING PLACES

When sisters go on vacation, they need no destination.

One hot, sunny day my sisters and I decided to go to the beach. When we got there, it was very crowded with people. First we set up our beach umbrella. Next we laid our towels on the sand. Last we put on sunscreen and got in the water. Before long my little sister, Nora, scrambled out of the water screaming, "Faith! There's a crab in my bathing suit!"

☞

Kellie is three years older than I am. She, of course, learned to read before I did. When our family went on vacation to California, she found a clever way to get our dad to stop at all the souvenir shops. When she saw a souvenir shop sign, she would whisper, "Tell Mom and Dad you have to go to the bathroom." So I began shouting that I had to go really bad. When we pulled off at the "Souvenir Village" or the "Indian Teepee," we looked at all the stuff and forgot we had to go to the bathroom. Mom or Dad would say, "I thought you had to go to the bathroom!" I think we were halfway from Memphis to California before they figured out what we were doing. They always thought I was the mischievous one, but Kellie has her moments.

☞

My sisters and I were always athletic. Although we never competed against each other in sports, every summer we would hold our arms together to see who had the darkest tan.

When my sisters, Lynn and Tricia, join us on vacation at the beach, we always buy lots of rafts and all kinds of inflatable toys—Shamu the whale, alligators, lobsters and any other kind of float we can find. But when we go down to the beach, nobody wants to carry them. Last year we could barely get through the door of the condo because all the floats, rafts and rings were on the front porch. I guess our family vacation wouldn't be the same without them.

ॐ

What a vacation it was! My four sisters and our mother spent a week at Bethany Beach, New Jersey. After being relieved of our baby-sitting duties, my sister Camille and I set out on our rafts.

The beach was patrolled by lifeguards, and buoys marked the swimming area. We had swum about 50 yards when crazy Camille stripped off her swimsuit and began skinny-dipping. I kept telling her people were looking. She insisted they couldn't see. About five minutes later, the lifeguard started waving for us to come in. Camille had to put on her wet swimsuit, so it took us awhile. I was the first to approach the lifeguard, with my sister about 200 feet behind. The lifeguard said he was motioning for us to come in because we had gone out too far. I asked him to tell my sister she was going to be assessed a fine for skinny-dipping. He agreed and I continued along, staying within earshot. When my sister reached the lifeguard, he asked if she knew it was against the law to swim naked in the ocean. She said, "No, the ocean belongs to everyone, and it is my free will to swim naked if I want." He told her that in accordance with the law he would have to fine her $500. Camille couldn't believe this and was outraged. Unable to contain myself I burst out laughing, along with others who had overheard.

Photos, maps and souvenirs … Are we there yet?

READING, WRITING & SISTER TRICKS

Reading, Writing & Sister Tricks

What did your sister teach you?

One winter night during high school, my sister stayed up very late studying for a test. After she finished her studies, she ran into my room screaming, "Get up! Get up! We're late for school!" After I was completely dressed and ready for school, I realized it was 3 a.m. and my sister was laughing hysterically.

ॐ

Being the youngest of three sisters, my two older sisters, Dreda and Virginia, would walk me to school each morning. I remember pretending to be sick on several occasions because Dreda, the oldest, was too ill to go to school, and I was certain Ginny would never be able to remember the way.

ॐ

When Cheryl and I were in high school, we were in the same study hall. The study hall was held in the auditorium to accommodate the large number of students. We were seated in alphabetical order, so my seat was right behind Cheryl's.

I got the hiccups in study hall one day and couldn't get rid of them. Cheryl whispered to me, "Open your mouth as wide as you can and hold your breath. Your hiccups will go away." I believed her. On the next hiccup, my mouth was like a megaphone. That hiccup shook walls, rolled pencils off desks, and awakened sleeping students. The monitoring teacher said, "Miss Rule, if you can't control your mannerisms, I will ask you to leave this study hall." Everyone could tell by my obvious blush to which Miss Rule he was referring.

I am the one who tried to teach my baby sister, Diane, to ride a bicycle. I had her sit on the seat while I pedaled and steered. My hands were on the handlebars, and my feet were on the pedals. Diane just sat on the seat with her arms and legs dangling. When I got up enough speed, I said to Diane, "Okay, get ready to ride!" At that moment, I just jumped off the back of the bicycle.

ॐ

I have always been attracted to the noble profession of education. I decided to put my phonics books to good use by teaching my younger sister, Elizabeth, to read. I was in the second grade at a Catholic school, so I knew exactly how school was supposed to be. First, I rummaged through the house searching for ugly and uncomfortable clothes. These were to be her uniform. I chose my closet for the classroom, and, of course, she would also need a desk. In my closet there were three shelves. The middle shelf was made from two boards, so I removed the back board and put Elizabeth in the shelves. Voilá–a perfect desk. I gave her the books, closed the door, and like any 10-year-old at 2 o'clock on a weekday, headed downstairs to watch the afternoon cartoons. Several hours later, Dreda heard someone knocking in my room. When she went to investigate, she found Elizabeth meekly calling, "Hey, I'm finished. Let me out please." Despite the cruel treatment, it seemed to work. Before she went to kindergarten, she had learned to read.

ॐ

When Marlene was in kindergarten, she decided to take our cat, Stripey, to school for show and tell. Stripey was a mean and nasty cat—the kind that gives cats a bad name. In the car on the way to school, the cat went wild and climbed the ceiling. When Marlene opened the car door to get out, Stripey took off. He was definitely not into show and tell. My sister was devastated. What was she going to do? She couldn't go to school with nothing for show and tell. My mother suggested that she take me, her little sister, instead of the cat. Marlene had no choice. My mother spent the day gallivanting without children, pleased with her brilliant idea for show and tell.

Throughout high school, mornings around our house were never easy. As a first child with a type A personality, I wanted to leave at a certain time to get "my" parking space. The only problem was my younger, type B personality sister. She would roll out of bed at the last minute only to find she had nothing to wear. Invariably, she would end up in my closet and eventually in my clothes. On one of these mornings, I couldn't take it any more. I marched in to tell my mother. Her response was, "Just handle it!" So I informed Tricia that she could not ride to school with me if she didn't take off my clothes. She would not comply. We raced to my car, and I locked her out. (I was handling it!) As I pulled out of the driveway, she jumped on the hood of the car. My response was to accelerate to the end of the driveway, slam on my brakes and fling her into the yard. Then I proceeded to school. (I handled it!)

Sisters don't always go by the book.

A Pain Just The Same

A PAIN JUST THE SAME

What's bugging you?

Hello, my name is Kelly. My little sister's name is Lindsay. When we went to Disney World, she was such a pain because she was whining and crying about being hot in Florida. I whined a little bit, too, but not as much as she did. One night we were all getting ready for bed when Lindsay started to scream and yell while she was in the bathtub. We all jumped up and headed toward the bathroom. We saw that she had lots of blood all over her. I was really scared! We saw Mom's razor lying on the side of the tub, and we knew what she had done. Mom got her cleaned up, and we put Band-aids on her cuts. Even though she had been a pain on the trip, I realized that I loved her and I didn't want anything to happen to her. She's still a pain at times, but I think I'll keep her.

ༀ

Hi, my name is Lindsay. Ever since I was born, all I heard was twin this and twin that. You see, I have twin sisters that are two years older than I. Wherever we went, the twins got all the attention. I did not like this, so when I was 2, I decided to tell people I was a twin also. I did not even know what being a twin meant, all I knew was that I wanted some attention, too. My mom knew that I was too little to understand about all the excitement twins caused, so she started calling me her "special single." After that, everywhere we went my sisters still got attention for being twins, but Mom always made sure everyone knew I was her "special single." Pretty soon my sisters began to tell everyone that I was their "special single sister." I don't think I need to be a twin anymore. I'm happy just being me!

When my family moved out of state, I was 16; my sister, Tara, was 15; and the youngest, Dana, was only 7. Since Tara and I were in our teens, we were really cool, and as far as we were concerned, Dana was nothing but a pest. I soon learned my true feelings.

About a week after we moved into our new house, one of the workmen who was applying the finishing touches to the house let our dog out of the yard. Dana started playing with the dog and followed him as he went to explore his new surroundings. Fifteen minutes later, we realized that the dog was gone and so was Dana. I don't think I've ever been so scared in my life. My little sister was gone!

We immediately began scouring the neighborhood, knocking on doors and searching everywhere. Mom jumped in the car and Tara and I were on bikes, while our brother stayed by the phone. After about 30 minutes of searching, we were ready to call the police. The waiting was killing me, so I took off on my bike one last time. As I rode around my new surroundings, all I could think about was how much I loved my little sister and that if we did find her she could pester me whenever she liked. About that time, I turned a corner and looked into the distance. I saw a lady pushing a stroller, walking with a young girl and a golden retriever. It was Dana! The woman was trying to help her find her way home. Within seconds, my mother came along in the car and we all had a joyous reunion. I never realized until that moment exactly how much my little sister meant to all of us.

She may have been a pest, but we never called the exterminator.

TEAMMATES FOR LIFE

TEAMMATES FOR LIFE

All for one and one for all. Who's there to pick you up when you fall?

I'm 6 years old and my name is Jackie. My best friend is my sister, Olivia. She is 5 years old. People think we are twins sometimes because we look alike and we dress alike. We like to help each other when it's hard to ask Mommy or Daddy something. One time Olivia got into trouble, and she wasn't allowed to have cookies after dinner. She asked me to get her some. When I asked Mommy for dessert, I took extras out of the cookie jar for both of us. We went out on the porch and ate them together. My mommy never found out! Sometimes Olivia does nice things for me, too. She tells Daddy she is scared of the dark and she wants to sleep in my bed. (I'm really the one who gets scared, but she doesn't mind asking for me.) He says okay, and we play with our flashlights in the dark until we fall asleep.

৵

Hi, my name is Kristen. I am a twin and proud of it. My twin sister, Kelly, is nine minutes older than I am. People think because we look alike and dress alike that we think alike. Well, one rainy day, Kelly and I were thinking alike. While my mom was asleep and my dad was watching TV, we sneaked out of the house while it was raining cats and dogs. Then we played and played until we were soaked. We had a great time. I guess you could say, "Great minds think alike."

When Aline was in high school and I was in junior high, we developed our own secret language–talking backward from the ends of sentences, changing the phonics as we went along. Thus, I was Notsag Hteb Yram and she was Notsag Enila. This put us in hysterics. One day one of us translated, "Eltrut wen a sah Divad," as "David has a new tootrle." Tootrle became the accepted pronunciation for turtle from that day forward.

ॐ

My sister and I always giggle when we are together. We are especially prone to laughter when we try to exercise any cooperation or coordination. Take, for instance, moving furniture. We will pick up the chair to move it downstairs. Halfway down, one of us can't help but look at the other. It's all over! In the end, the chair has to be put down, and we giggle until our sides hurt. Wallpaper is another scary story. Let's just say "straight" may not be the best final description, but we have fun. We have even been caught giggling in church.

ॐ

As sisters, we've always been willing to do whatever is necessary to help each other in times of need. On this occasion, Claire really needed our help. Her Junior prom happened to fall on the same day as our brother's wedding. As a member of the wedding party, Claire felt obliged to partake of the champagne being offered to the other guests. At 16, she wasn't aware of how quickly a few glasses of bubbly can go to one's head. This became obvious several hours later, as we tried to awaken her from a "deep sleep." Her date had arrived, and my sisters and I were trying to dress her. As one of us applied her makeup, the others helped her into her pantyhose and dress. On this particular evening, Claire was the one in need, and we all pitched in to help.

Sisterhood–you never have to try out for the team.

BELIEVE IT OR NOT

※

BELIEVE IT OR NOT

Brothers-in-law, holy water, Winnie the Pooh ... Is that a coincidence, too?

My baby sister is nine years younger than I am. She and I looked the most alike. None of us knew in 1988, when I got married, that six years later she would marry my husband's brother, who happens to look remarkably like my husband. I can't wait to see if their kids look like ours.

✌

My sister, Honey, was in town for Christmas. When she entered my bedroom, she exclaimed, "Gina, when did you get this new comforter? I bought this same set in Texas." Somehow we are in sync. The next year we sent each other the exact same Christmas card.

✌

I was born on my sister's fourth birthday. During the birthday picnic, my mother was taken to the hospital. My sister exclaimed when I was born, "This is the best birthday present ever, a little sister." By the time I was 3, my aunt says, she had retracted that statement and replaced it with "I wish she would hurry and grow up, so everyone wouldn't think she's so cute."

✌

Our one brother commented upon seeing a photograph of his four sisters at a bridal shower, "Don't you think there is something missing?" He, of course, meant himself.

As a young, innovative girl, Dreda showed her prowess as an entrepreneur on several occasions. During a visit with our devout Catholic aunt, she was given some holy water. Dreda asked if you have to go to Rome to get more holy water when you run out. My aunt told her that she simply saved a little of the holy water and added more water to it, then all the water would be blessed. Dreda took her little vial of water and, with a glimmer in her eye, headed home. Collecting all the containers we could find, from milk jugs to Coke bottles, we filled them up with water and put one drop of holy water in each. Placing all the jars in her closet, she intended to make a killing after Mass the next Sunday.

⚜

On Mother's Day 1994, our families gathered at our parent's home for Sunday lunch. My sister had called me three days earlier to tell me that I was going to be an aunt again. She already had a 3-year-old daughter, and I had two sons, 7 and 9 years old. We were all excited about the prospect of another baby in the family.

My husband asked the blessing before our meal. At the end of the prayer, he said, "And Lord, thank you for the *two* new additions to our family." I've never seen Lara more surprised. I had known since Easter that I was expecting, but my husband and I had decided to wait before making the announcement. You should always expect the unexpected when you are expecting.

⚜

At age 3, in 1968, my favorite character was Winnie the Pooh. Twenty-one years later, who but Pooh would be my sister, Ashlee's, favorite bear.

I have two sisters, Linda and Carolynn. At some point, two of the three of us were blondes. Linda has been true to her roots and remained a brunette. She has a picture of the three of us on her desk at work. Someone inquired about the photograph. Linda said, "These are my sisters." She was then asked why she colored her hair. She said, *"I don't, they do!"* As of this writing, I am the only sister that is not a brunette. Perhaps someday I will go back to my roots.

One day, I was getting on the elevator at work. A friend and I were talking about funny human tricks. I said, "My sister can fit her whole fist in her mouth." About that time, a guy in the back of the elevator said, "Wow! I'd really like to meet her."

Who needs the psychic hot line when you can call your sister?

EXCELLENT ADVENTURES

EXCELLENT ADVENTURES

When is it safe to listen to your sister?

My sister, Gwen, and I are completely different. Aside from the fact that she is 15 years older than I, Gwen's life is always organized, whereas mine is usually in disarray. I fly by the seat of my pants, and Gwen flies along a planned course. So you can imagine my surprise (and delight) the day Gwen pulled a "SaraJane."

My husband and I were moving our small family to a new state. My folks came to help us move, and since Gwen only lived 20 miles away, she decided to come help, too. We lived in one of those neighborhoods where most every house on every street looked the same. Gwen pulled into the driveway and proceeded into the house. As she walked down the hall, she persistently called, "Mother? Mother!" She walked into the bedroom and came face to face with a strange man. Right behind her, a woman was asking, "Honey, who is this woman?" The strange man said, "I don't know, but she is looking for her mother." With no hesitation and no explanation, my sister turned and fled out the door. She drove one street over and into my driveway. We've never let her live it down.

❧

When you are the baby of the family, you get blamed for a lot out of convenience. I can remember one time in my sister's and my childhood that I was glad to be the baby. My sister decided that she wanted to go to "the ditch." It was off-limits for many reasons. Being the little sister, I tagged along with the promise that I would not tell if I got to go. We had just crossed the busy street, climbed the fence and walked down to the water, when out of nowhere, our mother appeared. My sister got the blame for this one, and even more so because she took "the baby" with her.

My two sisters have always teased me about being so bossy. When we were young, we would walk to the park with friends in the afternoon. One day, one of the older girls in the neighborhood decided that we should take the shortcut across the rickety old plank bridge that crossed a large ravine. When we approached the bridge, I could tell that the boards were old and rotted. It just wasn't safe. I remember the older girl saying, "Come on, Ray Sisters. You're not afraid?" After much coercion, I finally convinced my sisters to take the long way around the ditch. The next week there was a tragic accident on that same bridge.

I'm not so sure how closely they heed my advice on other matters now that we are adults, but they still remember that their bossy sister knows best.

⁂

When we were growing up, my sister and my father often butted heads with one another. Both had red hair and possessed the fiery tempers often attributed to redheads.

On one occasion when they had clashed, my sister decided to run away from home. For some unknown reason, she also decided to take me with her. My sister was three years older than I, at least a foot taller, and very adept at bossing me around. So I went, cowardly little sister that I was at age 7.

We walked some hundred yards down the gravel road from our house to the railroad tracks. As my sister turned onto the tracks, my heart sank. This was forbidden territory. The previous fall, a truck full of cotton pickers was hit at a crossing, and they were all killed.

My sister marched resolutely down the tracks; I followed, my bony knees knocking together in fear. We walked closer to the dreaded trestle, where there would be no escape should a train come toward us.

My brain feebly considered my options. There was no doubt whatsoever in my mind that a train would most certainly come upon us should we venture onto the trestle. If I followed my sister, I would surely meet sudden death by a head-on collision with engine Number Nine or by my desperate, suicidal leap into the ravine deep below.

Not only would I die, I would go to hell on top of everything else; after all, I was directly disobeying my parents, and the Ten Commandments said not to do that. Mama and Daddy and God were all going to be mad at me! Of course, my only other option was to defy my sister and meet certain death at her hands.

Suddenly, I turned and broke into a terrified run toward home. "I'm going ho-o-ome," I yelled over my shoulder. Once pointed homeward, my legs worked remarkably well, as I raced back over the wooden railroad ties and gravel.

"Come back here, you little coward!" my sister screamed. As I glanced back over my shoulder, I could see her face scarlet with rage, most unbecoming next to her bright red hair. Then she began to chase after me, murder and mayhem in her eyes.

It's amazing how inspiring fear can be, especially if you are running for your life. For once, in spite of my lesser size and strength, I beat my sister. I could almost feel the heat of her angry breath on the back of my neck as I crashed through the back door of our house, running straight into my mother.

"Where have you girls been?" she asked. "Out," said my sister. Muddy sweat trickled down her face as she glared at me. Then she stomped into our room and slammed the door.

In spite of all my fear and anxiety, my sister never did seek revenge for my deserting her on that day. I think that secretly she wanted an excuse to come home, too. We never have spoken of that day to each other, and neither of us ever ran away from home again.

When sisters get together, it's always "risky business."

ALL DRESSED UP & NO PLACE TO GO

All Dressed Up & No Place To Go

Is that what you're wearing?

When my sister Liz and her husband were first married, he couldn't understand why she would lend her clothes to her sisters. He obviously had not grown up in a household where everything was shared, especially clothes.

I can remember going shopping and buying an item that I knew would go perfectly with one sister's blouse or another sister's skirt. Technically, the individual articles had an owner. I suppose this was important if ownership rights had to be imposed in order to get to wear a particular item. For the most part, we had the attitude, "What's mine is yours, and more importantly, what's yours is mine."

৯৯

When my sisters and I were younger, my mother would occasionally drag us all to K-Mart. We kept ourselves occupied playing video games, reading teen mags and having our picture made in the minute-photo booth.

৯৯

On more than one occasion when shopping with my sister, we have called to each other simultaneously from across the floor, "Look at this," only to turn and find each other holding up the same dress.

A good sense of humor becomes a necessity when sisters share the responsibilities of caring for aging parents. Because of our mother's health, she is unable to wash her laundry herself. One afternoon I picked up our mother's dirty clothes to take them home and wash. When I returned home, my washing machine was in need of repair. Luckily, I was planning to have dinner with my sisters that evening to celebrate one sister's birthday, so I put the dirty clothes in my car. After dinner, Dinky followed me to my car to get the clothes. The next day, she washed the clothes but didn't have time to take them back to Mom's before work. So Ann, who happens to work near Dinky, picked up the clean clothes and took them to her house, where they stayed for the remainder of the week. I later had to do major investigative work to determine the whereabouts of Mother's clothes.

❧

I can remember seeing a friend of my older sister, Rozzy, walking down the street wearing my favorite white midriff blouse. As I passed her on my banana-seat bicycle, I shouted, "Hey, that's my blouse!". She replied, "No it's not. Your sister Rozzy gave it to me. It's mine now."

Quick, call the fashion police. Put out an APB on my sister. She's wearing my new white blouse.

Insert Your Sister's Portrait Here

Write your sister story in the space provided below.

If you have a sister story that you would like considered for future editions of <u>Sister Stories</u>, please write it down and send it, with your address, telephone number and snapshot, to: Tricia Eleogram, 666 Hawthorne, Memphis, TN 38107.

Top Ten Reasons To Show Appreciation For Your Sister(s)

10.   No one can imitate your mother better.

9.   She can always be counted on in an emergency.

8.   No one else can get away with saying, "Those jeans make your butt look huge!"

7.   She knows where the silverware drawer should be located.

6.   You may need an organ donor one day.

5.   She won't let anyone, besides herself, criticize you.

4.   She knows how a towel should be folded.

3.   She'll take your side even when you're wrong.

2.   Since you are no longer living under the same roof, she can't borrow and ruin your favorite skirt without asking.

1.   All sisters turn into their mother eventually.

Acknowledgements

This book would not have been possible without the participation of the following sisters:

Marsha Alexander, Gina Andreuccetti, Theresa Andreuccetti, Robin Barrow, Geri Beaugrand, Jill Beck, Stacey Berry, Kay Bracato, Sharri Bruce, Martha Burks, Marlene Chapman, Elizabeth Collins, Etheldreda Collins, Joyce Crain, Sharon Cruthirds, Julie Crye, Claire Cunningham, Jackie Currie, Olivia Currie, Kelly Davidson, Kristen Davidson, Dinky Delisi, Sara Jane Dillard, Molly Duggan, Irene Dycus, Mary Eleogram, Gina Epperson, Donna Fennell, Ellen Flynn, Lou Ann Goad, Rosalind Golden, Aubrey Guy, Denise Haney, Sue Harrison, Jill Hartsfield, Joanne Helming, Diane Hopkins, Elizabeth Horton, Claire Hyrka, Kathy Johnson, Rosalie Johnson, Linda Jones, Merlynn Kassing, Cheryl Kent, Velma Lamar, Claudia Laws, Diane Lee, Pat Lenoir, Elizabeth Lovejoy, Kellie Lowrey, Sharon Lundquist, Claudia Lyons, Grace Ann Mabry, Paula May, Lara McKinley, Carolynn McMahan, Linda McMahan, Anna McNair, Lisa McNinch, Mary Messenger, Ann Murphy, Lynn Nelson, Gwen O'Banon, Faith Orono, Hope Orono, Nora Orono, Camille Palazola, Jo Jo Palazola, Louise Palazola, Pam Palazola, Carol Payne, Ali Powell, Barbara Ray, Amy Richter, Ann Riggs, Ashlee Rivalto, Mandy Rodgers, Margaret Rucker, Aline Russell, Virginia Russell, Mary Schoggen, Virginia Shingleton, Mary Spencer, Janet Staunton, Shelley Stracener, Elaine Stroud, Phyllis Taylor, Thedora Taylor, Caren Vandergrift, Mary Vanderpool, Lorie Vital, Lynn Wade, Amy Webster, Holly Webster, Susan Wells, Rita West, Frankie Whitmore, Tara Wilson, Elise Woodmansee, Elizabeth Woodmansee, Jenifer Wright, Susan Wyatt, Dana Zanone, Monica Zanone.

Special thanks to:

Mike Rivalto, Randall Bedwell, Rik Berry, David Eleogram, Palmer Jones, Olivia Miller, Jil Foutch, H. Jackson Brown, Bob Chandler, Stephen, Zach, Eli and Mason.

Tricia Eleogram lives in Memphis, Tennessee, where she teaches first grade at Shannon Elementary. Her sisters, Lynn and Ashlee, were the inspiration for this book. "Life without sisters would be like life without music," says Eleogram. She is president of the Sisters' Day Council and is responsible for the establishment of Sisters' Day. Tricia encourages sisters worldwide to celebrate the spirit of sisterhood each August.

Stacey Berry lives in Memphis, Tennessee, with her husband, Rik, and two sons, Zachary and Eli. She owns and operates Partners In Design, a small graphics design studio. Her sister, Kellie Lowrey, is not only a devoted friend but a terrific aunt, who always has gum. It is Stacey's hope that as sisters share this book, they will remember special moments of their own and smile.

Louise Palazola is a portrait artist who has done extensive studies in women's portraiture. She resides in Escondido, California, where she raises her young son, Mason, and operates Palazola Photography. Her main concentrations are environmental portraits and fine art photography. Louise has a fine arts degree from the University of Denver and exhibits her work throughout the United States. As her son, Mason, has watched the many stages of this book, he has asked, "When is Mommy going to do a book about me?"